Dishcloth

diva

dishcloth diva

Library of Congress Control Number: 2012949836
ISBN 13: 978-1-937513-14-6
First Cooperative Press edition
Published by http://www.cooperativepress.com

Every effort has been made to ensure that all the information in this book is accurate at the time of publication; however, Cooperative Press neither endorses nor guarantees the content of external links referenced in this book.

If you have questions or comments about this book, or need information about licensing, custom editions, special sales, or academic/corporate purchases, please contact Cooperative Press: info@cooperativepress.com or 13000 Athens Ave C288, Lakewood, OH 44107 USA.

for cooperative press

Senior Editor: Shannon Okey
Assistant Editor: Elizabeth Green Musselman

Technical Editor: Joeli Caparco

Contents

Foreword
by kay gardiner

"What are you making?"

I knit on trains, planes and in automobiles. This tends to attract the attention of my fellow travelers. They often announce that I am crocheting, and I've learned that they do not want to be corrected. They know what I'm doing. What they want to know is, what am I making?

I hate that question. Because what I am knitting is, very often, a dishcloth.

I'm a grownup. I'm a feminist. I read. I write. I keep up on Current Events. I can sight-sing. Somehow, acknowledging to a stranger that I'm knitting a dishcloth—something so humble, so connected to traditional "women's work," which can be purchased at any supermarket, usually for less than two dollars—is embarrassing. It seems like I should have something better to do with my time.

But I love knitting dishcloths. Dishcloths are the savory snacks of knitting. They are a respite from sweaters that stall, inexplicably, at the second sleeve, a sanity-preserving haven from lace shawls that are missing a single stitch in one of 19 repeats of the pattern, and you have to find out where it is, and fish that stitch back up again.

Dishcloths are more than just an escape; they are a destination unto themselves. On the small screen of a dishcloth, a knitter can play with color and pattern, try out new techniques, and even take the first tentative steps toward designing. Dishcloth cotton is cheap enough to keep on hand in every color you like, and some you don't like, just to play around. And since all dishcloths fade to colorlessness with repeated use and laundering, it's OK to make an ugly one now and then—time is the great equalizer. That hole slightly left of center?—that's a design feature.

Some knitters like dishcloths so much that they devote almost all of their knitting time to churning them out. You drop by their house for a cup of coffee, they give you a dishcloth. You renovate your kitchen, they give you a set of six dishcloths to match the new backsplash. Your nephew gets into the University of Michigan, they give you a map of Michigan, in dishcloth form. The problem for these knitters: running out of dishcloth patterns.

That's where a book like this one comes in. A whole new collection of textured dishcloth patterns, beautifully presented. It will keep a lot of dishcloth knitters out of trouble, on a lot of subway rides. Enjoy, and don't be afraid to tell people what you're making.

—Kay Gardiner is co-author, with Ann Shayne, of two popular knitting books, Mason-Dixon Knitting *and* Mason-Dixon Knitting Outside the Lines, *both of which feature dishcloths and other items for the home. Find her every day at www.masondixonknitting.com, yakking about her knitting passions of the moment.*

Introduction from the Girl Next Door

by deb buckingham

I truly am the girl next door. You know, the one you go have coffee with, or the one you call and say, "Hey, there's a great sale on yarn, wanna go?"

Yep, I'm there.

Since I come from a family of knitters, including my mom and grandma, knitting was obviously something I'd do ONE day. As a girl growing up, I undeniably had other things on my mind: boys, hanging out with my friends, *more boys*, and reading. It wasn't until I became an adult with kids and a series of jobs behind me that it grew obvious I was on the road to something fun via knitting. Knitting as a career!

I was a young mom who took my job seriously. My husband never told me I had to find a job outside the home, though I knew in my heart that my need for people contact was a must, and that sales would be the perfect fit for my outgoing personality. So, I set out to find a picture-perfect sales job, which led to positions with several direct sales companies. They seemed the right fit for me at the time. Getting out of the house at night to throw a "party" where I could have adult conversation with lots of other women was my thing—never mind that I got to sell them stuff, too.

That grew old after several years and I realized that having a regularly scheduled, part-time job outside the house when my husband was home just might fill my need for social contact. I worked in a Hallmark store for a while... then became anxious to leave. You can see a trend happening here, right?

Heading back to the Full-Time Mom role, I felt whole again. I found much satisfaction in moms' mornings out where I was able to do things that fulfilled me. We ended up moving to Colorado, and life was comfortable.

I was still searching for that "perfect" job for me... one that would allow me to have conversations with adults, rather than children. After searching the help wanted ads, I discovered a course in CNA (Certified Nurse Aide) training. I signed up to take the four-week course and felt I was on the road to something great; something that would fulfill that need to be with people, and allow me to feel independent without having to constantly entertain young people. After many long hours studying, and plenty of nervous moments, I knew in my heart that I wanted to work with terminally ill patients in hospice. Having watched many family members go through the hospice program, it seemed a perfect fit.

Life was good.

After spending six nourishing years as a nursing assistant for hospice patients, I soon realized there was (still) much more to life. I loved being a nurse and talking with my patients and their families about their lives, but dealing with death every day made me stop and think really hard about what *I* needed once again. Passion and love for my job and my patients just weren't enough.

Sound selfish? Not really. The dying process is something everyone goes through in their lifetime, but it wasn't something I cared to deal with on a daily basis anymore.

I put in my two-week notice and left, feeling satisfied and empty at the same time.

Our kids were older now. They had their own friends (not just mom), and their own daily routines. My supportive, adorable, and loving husband knew I was still searching for my own identity. I started to explore and develop my skills via both knitting and writing.

I taught myself to knit through friends, YouTube videos, books and knitting groups. I became a knitting instructor, and then a designer. My love for the craft grew daily. Some called me a knit-a-holic (and still do), or even a yarn snob (most days), because the moment I found myself face to face with the luxury yarns, I was hooked and still am. I have it bad, I know.

I wrote my first novel sitting in a coffee shop over the course of nine months. The characters grew into my friends. Weird, huh? Nah, I loved how they developed and often talked with my husband about them as if they *were* my friends. He got

it. He got me. And since starting down this path I've been able to combine my love of both writing and knitting.

Knitting is something that can consume my day, and often does. I love a challenging project, though that hasn't always been the case. A simple knit-and-purl pattern is my go-to project every time, and that's where I began as a novice knitter. Knitting these simple projects gives me the courage to tackle more complex patterns—a pattern with cables, for example, or maybe color work.

My desire is for you, the reader, to feel my passion for knitting through these designs. They're simple, modern patterns that any knitter can accomplish successfully. Drawing on my experience as a quilter, my knitted dishcloth patterns transform simple shapes and lines into something with modern flair.

I'm your average girl next door, with the same day-to-day struggles and desires that we all experience… but now I'm living my dream, and truly feel blessed.

Thanks for picking up this book. I hope you find time to sit down and knit a bit, because that morsel of time you take for yourself will bring much comfort to your day.

—Deb

All About Cotton

For decades, knitters have used cotton to knit dishcloths. Why not? It's the most absorbent and easy to find yarn that's just right for a knitted washcloth.

Some knitters find cotton hard to knit with because it can be thick and not slide well on the needles. I get that. Others ask why would you even want to knit with cotton? They aren't sure why they should consider it. Or maybe they haven't had an opportunity to try it.

Others, like me, love cotton for its versatility. Typically, cotton is a fiber that everyone can use (no allergens to worry about), and clearly it's a major reason why we all love our t-shirts and comfy jeans. Cotton *is* all that!

I find myself drawn to cotton, all different kinds of cotton. My daily mission is to see what "other" cottons are out there, so I can buy them, bring them home, and knit with them. What I discovered was that not all cottons play alike, and not all cottons work for dishcloths.

For instance: you'd think flour is flour, right? It's not. Cake flour used in a recipe that calls for all-purpose flour will not yield the same result. All-purpose flour, as its name states, is used for general baked goods such as cookies, breads or biscuits. Cake flour is milled specifically for cakes to give them the right texture and make them softer. All-purpose flour has a hard texture. Cake flour is finely ground. All-purpose flour contains a higher protein content, which means more gluten, resulting in a dense texture. Cake flour has less protein, meaning less gluten, resulting in softer products.

How's that for your flour lesson?

Now, how about cotton?

Cotton yarns are labeled in many different descriptive ways, from mercerized to organic to USA-grown to just plain "cotton." Detailed labels tell you exactly what you're getting.

Let's start with mercerized cotton.

Mercerized cotton yarn has been put through a process to increase luster. This process makes it stronger, smoother, and shinier than regular cotton. If you like the shine, this is definitely the cotton fiber for you. It's a perfect blend for kitchen knitting use. Its soda bath treatment (mercerization) increases its strength, allowing for tons of scrubbing. The process also shrinks the cotton fibers, tightening and smoothing the grain of the thread. Because mercerized cotton is preshrunk, it won't shrink as much as regular cotton. It wears for years.

Let's take Tahki Cotton Classic (my favorite mercerized cotton yarn) as an example. I find I need to go up a needle size to get a larger sized dishcloth. This particular cotton is a DK weight. It's typical to get 5 sts/inch on a size 6 needle, so if you go up to a size 7 needle, you will get about 4.5 sts/inch.

What about organic cotton?

Organic cotton is *the* big trend right now in the plant fiber yarn world, and in my opinion, this trend has staying power. It's an eco-friendly product, making it perfect for those seeking natural fibers. It's usually grown in subtropical countries without the use of synthetic agricultural chemicals such as fertilizers or pesticides, giving it a lower impact on the environment unlike its non-organically grown counterparts.

How is it to work with 100% organic cotton, you ask? Well… it's just fabulous! Consider Classic Elite Verde's Seedling. *Oh. My. Gosh.* I love this cotton yarn! It has a bit of texture that makes it perfect for knitting dishcloths. It's soft and very easy to use, a worsted weight where you get about 4.5 sts/inch on a 7 size needle—the perfect combination.

How 'bout USA-grown cotton?

Here I mean the kitchen cottons that you can find in any chain craft store. They are by far the easiest to get your hands on and they're quite durable. Kitchen cotton works up quickly, but is somewhat thicker, so make sure your chosen needles are a bit slick. Everyone has their favorite. These cottons come in a full array of colors. Sugar and Cream or Peaches and Cream are two popular yarn kitchen cotton yarn brands that come to mind.

Plain 100% cotton yarn rocks!

My favorite is KnitPicks Dishie yarn. It's on the thinner side of worsted, but still knits up with ease and glides across your needles—just plain fabulous. And the colors? Plenty to choose from, in both solid and variegated colorways.

Cotton pros

- Cotton is a breathable, lightweight fiber that is great for summer clothing and accessories such as scarves and dishcloths.
- Cotton is machine-washable, durable and in some cases, gets softer with each washing.
- Cotton brings out the details of every stitch.

- It doesn't pill.
- It's inexpensive.

Cotton cons

- Cotton doesn't have elastic qualities, so tension may be an issue for some. You can swatch if you like; however, when making a dishcloth gauge really doesn't matter. You won't be wearing it, after all. Just remember to hold your yarn loosely enough to grab the yarn and tug gently to tighten, giving it a perfect tension.
- Some darker cotton yarn colors can fade and should be washed alone or with other dark colors so as to not run onto any lighter colors in a washing load.
- Cotton can get heavy when wet due to the amount of water it can hold.
- Cotton is super absorbent (but who wouldn't want that in a dishcloth?).

Cotton is an amazing fiber for dishcloths, but I would suggest a few things to think about when you're working with cotton. First, take breaks if you feel your hands are getting tired. Also, some cotton doesn't always slide easily on the needles, but using bamboo or coated needles will make your job a bit easier.

When knitting dishcloths, a 100% cotton fiber is recommended. Using a cotton blend isn't necessarily the best when knitting this kind of project. The absorbency rate of cotton blends falls sharply when used in a wiping-up-the-spills test. So grab your favorite 100% cotton yarn and your favorite needles for a fun, relaxing time with one of the patterns in this book. You'll find your stress level goes down several notches.

Knit on!

knotty or nice

pop of color

Decorating with neutral tones is fine, but adding a pop of color can rocket your space from drab to fab. Incorporating shades that complement the existing décor allows a tired space to come alive, adding a bit of sophistication. A red rug or blue throw pillow will draw the eye toward that pop of color rather than the overall beige or gray tones in the room. This dishcloth is a simple knit and works up well in multicolored yarns.

Finished Measurements

Approximately 8" / 20.5cm square
Note: Dimensions may vary depending on yarn used.

Materials

- Knit One, Crochet Too [100% cotton; 196 yds / 179m per 100g skein]; color: Oceana; 1 skein
- 1 set US #7 / 4.5mm needles, or size needed to obtain gauge
- Tapestry needle
- Scissors
- Row counter or stitch markers, if desired

Gauge

20 sts / 24 rows = 4" / 10cm in stockinette stitch

Pattern Notes

Included in the pattern directions is a k3 border on each end of the row. These are good places to add stitch markers, if you wish.

Directions

CO 41 sts.
Bottom border: Knit 3 rows.

Row 1 (RS): Knit all sts.
Row 2: Knit all sts.
Row 3: K3, k1, *sl 1 purlwise wyib, k1; rep from * to last 3 sts, k3.
Row 4: K3, k1, *yf, sl 1 purlwise, yb, k1; rep from * to last 3 sts, k3.

Rows 5 & 6: Knit all sts.
Row 7: K3, k2, *sl 1 purlwise wyib, k1; rep from * to last 4 sts, k1, k3.
Row 8: K3, k2, *yf, sl 1 purlwise, yb, k1; rep from * to last 4 sts, k1, k3.

Rep this 8-row pattern a total of 9 times.

Top border: Knit 4 rows.

Finishing

BO all sts and weave in all ends.

abstract

Abstract art in a room can make a subtle statement without overpowering the overall design. A great way to add an abstract note to any knit design is by working in colors from the opposite side of the color wheel; it adds contrast and challenged the mind's eye. It's fun to combine colors that you *like in a simple knit like this one. Grab a few different balls of yarn and knit away!*

Finished Measurements

Approximately 8.5" / 21.5cm square
Note: Dimensions may vary depending on yarn used.

Materials

- Lily Sugar and Cream Yarn [100% cotton; 120 yds / 110m per 70g skein]; color: Country Green; 1 skein
- 1 set US #6 / 4mm needles, or size needed to obtain gauge
- Tapestry needle
- Scissors
- Row counter or stitch markers, if desired

Gauge

18 sts / 24 rows = 4" / 10cm in stockinette stitch

Pattern Notes

Be careful when transitioning through the 4 rows; they look the same, but the sequence of stitches changes.

There is a k3 border on each end of row included in pattern directions.

Directions

CO 38 sts.
Bottom border: Knit 5 rows.

Row 1 (RS): K3, *k2, p2; rep from * to last 3 sts, k3.
Row 2: K3, *p2, k2; rep from * to last 3 sts, k3.
Row 3: K3, *p2, k2; rep from * to last 3 sts, k3.
Row 4: K3, *k2, p2; rep from * to last 3 sts, k3.

Rep this 4-row pattern a total of 14 times.

Top border: Knit 5 rows.

Finishing

BO all sts and weave in all ends.

sleek

Modern design is sleek and contemporary with clean lines, giving an overall streamlined and neatly tailored look. No magnets on the refrigerator. No knobs on the cabinets. Appliances all in the same finish, whether stainless steel or white porcelain. The rule in sleek design is to declutter the space as much as possible. When you're decorating in such a modern style, add a soft knit in a modern color like this one to bring life to your sink and keep the room from feeling cold!

Finished Measurements

Approximately 8" / 20.5cm square
Notes: Dimensions may vary depending on yarn used. This pattern has ribbing allowing the sides to relax a bit.

Materials

- Classic Elite Seedling [100% organic cotton; 110 yds / 101m per 50g skein]; color: Old Lavender; 1 skein
- 1 set US #7 / 4.5mm needles, or size needed to obtain gauge
- Tapestry needle
- Scissors
- Row counter or stitch markers, if desired

Gauge

16 sts / 24 rows = 4" / 10cm in stockinette stitch

Pattern Notes

There is a k3 border on each end of the row included in the pattern directions. A row counter is helpful with this pattern.

Directions

CO 36 sts.
Bottom border: Knit 4 rows.

Rows 1, 3 & 5 (WS): K3, *k2, p2; rep from * to last 5 sts, k2, k3.
Rows 2 & 4 (RS): K3, p2, *k2, p2; rep from * to last 3 sts, k3.
Row 6: K3, p2, *yo, skp, p2; rep to last 3 sts, k3.

Rep this 6-row pattern 8 times.

Top border: Knit 3 rows.

Finishing

BO all sts and weave in all ends.

glass

There's nothing like glass as a design element. Glass can be used in vases, tabletops, countertops, and backsplash accents. It allows the room to feel weightless and brings in more light and reflection. I love the look of a tiled backsplash with inserted glass tiles for added interest. But just like stainless steel, you might want to polish it up now and again. Try this simple cable washcloth for starters and you'll be ready to shine things up!

Finished Measurements

Approximately 6.5" / 16.5cm square
Note: Dimensions may vary depending on yarn used.

Materials

- Filatura Di Crosa Lovely Jeans [100% cotton; 93 yds / 85m per 50g skein]; color: #74; 1 skein
- 1 set US #7 / 4.5mm needles, or size needed to obtain gauge
- Cable needle
- Tapestry needle
- Scissors
- Row counter or stitch markers, if desired

Gauge

18 sts / 24 rows = 4" / 10cm in stockinette stitch

Pattern Notes

There is a k3 border on each end of the row included in the pattern directions. This is a crossed rib stitch.

Cr3B: Slip 2 sts onto cn and hold at back of work. K1, slip purl st from cn onto LH needle and purl it. K1 from cn.

Directions

CO 39 sts.
Bottom border: Knit 3 rows.

Row 1 & 3 (RS): K3, *p1, k1; rep from * to last 4 sts, p1, k3.
Row 2, 4 & 6 (WS): K3, k1, *p1, k1; rep from * to last 3 sts, k3.
Row 5: K3, *p1, Cr3B; rep from * to last 4 sts, p1, k3.

Rep this 6-row pattern a total of 6 times.

Top border: Knit 4 rows.

Finishing

BO all sts and weave in all ends.

stonework

Some modern kitchens have a stone backsplash. Stonework comes in all shapes and sizes, from chunky squares to elaborate, penny-sized subway tiles, and everything in between. Stonemasonry is the craft of forming pieces of rock into precise geometrical shapes. This pattern was instead modeled using yarn to create a simple arrangement of "stones" as geometric shapes.

Finished Measurements

Approximately 8" / 20.5cm square
Note: Dimensions may vary depending on yarn used.

Materials

- KnitPicks Dishie [100% cotton; 190 yds / 174m per 100g skein]; color: Aster; 1 skein
- 1 set US #7 / 4.5mm needles, or size needed to obtain gauge
- Tapestry needle
- Scissors
- Row counter or stitch markers, if desired

Gauge

18 sts / 24 rows = 4" / 10cm in stockinette stitch

Pattern Notes

There is a k3 border on each end of the row included in the pattern directions.

Directions

CO 34 sts.
Bottom border: Knit 3 rows.

Rows 1, 3, & 11 (RS): K3, *k4, p6, k4; rep from * to last 3 sts, k3.
Rows 2 & 12 (WS): K3, p28, k3.
Rows 4 & 10: K3, *p3, k1, p6, k1, p3; rep from * to last 3 sts, k3.
Rows 5 & 9: K3, *k2, p1, k8, p1, k2; rep from * to last 3 sts, k3.
Rows 6 & 8: K3, *p1, k1, p10, k1, p1; rep from * to last 3 sts, k3.
Row 7: K3, *p1, k12, p1; rep from * to last 3 sts, k3.

Rep this 12-row pattern 4 times.

Top border: Knit 4 rows.

Finishing

BO all sts and weave in all ends.

lines

linear

In modern design it seems everything is linear. Lines. Lines. Lines. Think of a long rectangular table, or how about elongated handles on sleek cabinets? It's both comfortable yet functional. Some might say it is cold, but remember: when you break up lines with other textures, you'll bring in added visual interest. This washcloth has a simple stitch that shows off its texture in well-defined rows of lines.

Finished Measurements

Approximately 7.5" / 19cm square
Note: Dimensions may vary depending on yarn used.

Materials

- Plymouth Yarn Fantasy Naturale [100% mercerized cotton; 140 yds / 128m per 100g skein]; color: #2574; 1 skein
- 1 set US #7 / 4.5mm needles, or size needed to obtain gauge
- Tapestry needle
- Scissors
- Row counter or stitch markers, if desired

Gauge

18 sts / 24 rows = 4" / 10cm in stockinette stitch

Pattern Notes

There is a k3 border on each end of the row included in the pattern directions.

Directions

CO 36 sts.
Bottom border: Knit 3 rows.

Row 1 (RS): Knit.
Row 2 (WS): K3, *k2tog; rep from * to last 3 sts, k3.
Row 3: K3, *kfb of each st; rep from * to last 3 sts, k3.
Row 4: K3, p30, k3.

Rep this 4-row pattern 11 times.

Top border: Knit 5 rows.

Finishing

BO all sts and weave in all ends.

Only the necessary elements are exposed in minimal designs, eliminating all non-essential features, forms, and details. In this design you really see the knit and purl stitches—the always-present elements in any knitting project—and their simplicity makes the design pop without interfering visually with the multi-colored yarn used. This is also a fun square to use for baby blankets and other projects that need to be reversible.

Finished Measurements

Approximately 9.5" / 24cm square
Note: Dimensions may vary depending on yarn used.

Materials

- Classic Elite Yarns Seedling [100% organic cotton; 110 yds / 101m per 50g skein]; color: #4567; 1 skein
- 1 set US #7 / 4.5mm needles, or size needed to obtain gauge
- Tapestry needle
- Scissors
- Row counter or stitch markers, if desired

Gauge

18 sts / 24 rows = 4" / 10cm in stockinette stitch

Pattern Notes

There is a k6 border on each end of the row included in the pattern directions.

This design was made to be larger for those that desire a larger dishcloth.

Directions

CO 44 sts.

Row 1 (WS): Knit.
Rows 2-14: Knit.
Row 15 and all odd-numbered rows through row 27: K6, p32, k6.
Row 16 and all even-numbered rows through row 28: Knit.
Rows 29-42: Knit.
Row 43 and all odd-numbered rows through row 55: K6, p32, k6.
Row 44 and all even-numbered rows through row 56: Knit.
Rows 57-70: Knit.

Finishing

BO all sts and weave in all ends.

stainless

Stainless steel adds elegance to any décor. Whether the room's look is contemporary or traditional, adding a stainless steel backsplash or countertop can add zing to a not-so-zing kitchen. But sometimes you need some soft color to offset cold steel: try knitting one of these cloths for the next time you need to polish fingerprints off that stainless steel fridge!

Finished Measurements

Approximately 8" / 20.5cm square
Note: Dimensions may vary depending on yarn used.

Materials

- Plymouth Yarns Fantasy Naturale [100% mercerized cotton; 140 yds / 128m per 100g skein]; color: #9005; 1 skein
- 1 set US #7 / 4.5mm needles, or size needed to obtain gauge
- Tapestry needle
- Scissors
- Row counter or stitch markers, if desired

Gauge

18 sts / 24 rows = 4" / 10cm in stockinette stitch

Pattern Notes

Included in the pattern directions is a k3 border on each end of the row. These are good places to add stitch markers, if you wish.

Directions

CO 40 sts.
Bottom border: Knit 3 rows.

Row 1 and all RS rows through 11: Knit.
Row 2 and all WS rows through 12: K3, p1, k2, *p4, k2; rep * to last 4 sts, p1, k3.
Row 13 and all RS rows through 23: Knit.
Row 14 and all WS rows through 24: K3, p4, *k2, p4; rep from * to last 3 sts, k3.

Rep this 24-row pattern once more.

Top border: Knit 4 rows.

Finishing

BO all sts and weave in all ends.

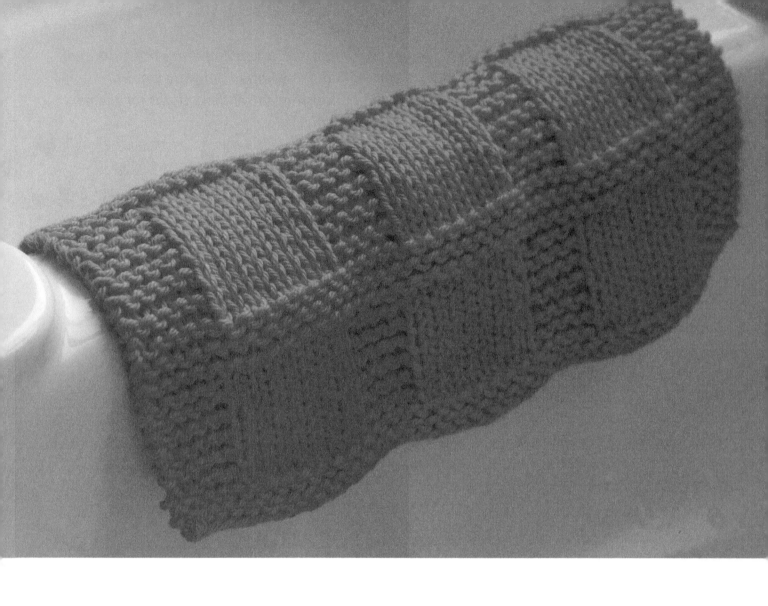

contemporary

Clean lines define contemporary style in all the trendy home décor magazines. I know that I can't walk into a bookstore without heading to the magazine section first. I'm drawn to the colors and the minimalistic approach in contemporary interior and clothing design. That neutral palette with an added pop of color is always candy to my eyes. Choose a rich color that's soothing to knit, as I've done here with a delicious shade of coral, and you'll have eye candy, too!

Finished Measurements

Approximately 9" / 23cm square
Note: Dimensions may vary depending on yarn used.

Materials

- KnitPicks Dishie [100% cotton; 190 yds / 174m per 100g skein]; color: Conch; 1 skein
- 1 set US #7 / 4.5mm needles, or size needed to obtain gauge
- Tapestry needle
- Scissors
- Row counter or stitch markers, if desired

Gauge

18 sts / 24 rows = 4" / 10cm in stockinette stitch

Pattern Notes

There is a k3 border on each end of the row included in the pattern directions.

Directions

CO 42 sts.
Bottom border: Knit 3 rows.

Row 1 (RS) and all odd-numbered rows through Row 11: Knit.
Row 2 (WS) and all even-numbered rows through Row 12: K5, (p8, k4) twice, p8, k5.
Row 13-18: Knit.

Rep this 18-row pattern 3 times, THEN rows 1-12 once more.

Top border: Knit 4 rows.

Finishing

BO all sts and weave in all ends.

neutrals

Neutral colors form a great backdrop for any decorating style. Woven chair backs add simple elegance to a neutral-colored dining room, and are reflected here in a stitch pattern that brings to mind organic textures such as leaves, turtle shells and rocks. Extended, this pattern would also make a lovely scarf.

Finished Measurements

Approximately 8.5" / 21.5cm square
Note: Dimensions may vary depending on yarn used.

Materials

- Tahki Yarns Sky [100% cotton; 96 yds / 88m per 50g skein]; color: Khaki; 1 skein
- 1 set US #6 / 4mm needles, or size needed to obtain gauge
- Tapestry needle
- Scissors
- Row counter or stitch markers, if desired

Gauge

20 sts / 24 rows = 4" / 10cm in stockinette stitch

Pattern Notes

Included in the pattern directions is a k3 border on each end of the row. These are good places to add stitch markers, if you wish.

Directions

CO 45 sts.
Bottom border: Knit 3 rows.

Row 1 (RS): Knit.
Row 2 (WS): K3, p39, k3.
Row 3: Knit.
Row 4: K3, p1, k11, *p2, k11; rep from * to last 4 sts, p1, k3.
Row 5: K3, k1, p11, *k2, p11; rep from * to last 4 sts, k1, k3.
Row 6: Rep Row 4.
Row 7: K3, k1, p2, k7, p2, *k2, p2, k7, p2; rep from * to last 4 sts, k1, k3.
Row 8: K3, p1, k2, p7, k2, *p2, k2, p7, k2; rep from * to last 4 sts, p1, k3.
Row 9: Rep Row 7.
Row 10: K3, p1, k2, p2, k3, *[p2, k2] twice, p2, k3; rep from * to last 8 sts, p2, k2, p1, k3.
Row 11: K3, k1, p2, k2, p3, *[k2, p2] twice, k2, p3; repeat from * to last 8 sts, k2, p2, k1, k3
Row 12: Rep Row 10.
Row 13: Rep Row 11.
Row 14: Rep Row 8.
Row 15: Rep Row 7.
Row 16: Rep Row 8.
Row 17: Rep Row 5.
Row 18: Rep Row 4.
Row 19: Rep Row 5.
Row 20: Rep Row 2.

Rep this 20-row pattern 3 times.

Top border: Knit 4 rows.

Finishing

BO all sts and weave in all ends.

rib it

clean lines

I've always been drawn to the clean lines in modern décor. An uncluttered look, with one major neutral color in the palette, forms the basis of modern style. You can also add a bold color throughout to enhance the palette, and allow for warmth. Still, neutral doesn't have to mean "boring"! Try a calming not-quite-beige-or-gray color like this Honeydew as a basis for your look.

Finished Measurements

Approximately 8" / 20.5cm square
Note: Dimensions may vary depending on yarn used. The ribbed effect allows for a more cinched in appearance on the side.

Materials

- KnitPicks Dishie [100% cotton; 190 yds / 174m per 100g ball]; color: Honeydew; 1 skein
- 1 set US #6 / 4mm needles, or size needed to obtain gauge
- Tapestry needle
- Scissors
- Row counter or stitch markers, if desired

Gauge

18 sts / 24 rows = 4" / 10cm in stockinette stitch

Pattern Notes

This pattern is reversible. There is a [k1, p1, k1] border on each end of row included in the pattern directions.

Directions

CO 37 sts.
Bottom border: Work [k1, p1] across for 3 rows (seed stitch).

Row 1 (RS): [K1, p1, k1], k3, *p1, k3; rep from * to last 3 sts, [k1, p1, k1].
Row 2 (WS): [K1, p1, k1], k1, *p1, k3; rep from * to last 5 sts, p1, k1, [k1, p1, k1].

Rep this 2-row pattern 25 times.

Top border: Work [k1, p1] across for 2 rows (seed stitch).

Finishing

BO all sts and weave in all ends.

new

Modern design offers new perspective, new vision, reinventing old styles with new ideas. It's a free-flowing, eco-friendly style with lots of natural light. Layered, with textures and warmth—a decorating style that's comfortable and unfussy. I love the textures, colors, and overall feel of a modern kitchen; a place to sit with friends. This dishcloth, knit in a vivid fuchsia, evokes those happy times.

Finished Measurements

Approximately 8" / 20.5cm square
Note: Dimensions may vary depending on yarn used.

Materials

- Classic Elite Yarns Seedling [100% organic cotton; 110 yds / 101m per 50g skein]; color: Vivid Fuchsia; 1 skein
- 1 set US #7 / 4.5mm needles, or size needed to obtain gauge
- Tapestry needle
- Scissors
- Row counter or stitch markers, if desired

Gauge

18 sts / 24 rows = 4" / 10cm in stockinette stitch

Pattern Notes

There is a k3 border on each end of the row included in the pattern directions.

Directions

CO 37 sts.
Bottom border: Knit 3 rows.

Row 1 (RS): Knit.
Row 2 (WS): K3, p31, k3.
Rows 3 & 4: Knit.

Repeat this 4-row pattern a total of 14 times.

Top border: Knit 2 rows.

Finishing

BO all sts and weave in all ends.

simple

There's nothing like freshening up a living space and making it feel new. A makeover can lift your mood and give your home an entirely new feel. Painting the walls, using slip covers on sofas, or sewing new accent pillows are all simple ideas to spice up a tired-looking room. Using DIY methods for these easy fixes saves time and money, and not much skill is required. (Not to mention that any of these patterns could easily be knit bigger and made into comfy new throw pillows!)

Finished Measurements

Approximately 8.5" / 21.5cm square
Note: Dimensions may vary depending on yarn used.

Materials

- Malabrigo 100% Organic Cotton [100% organic cotton; 232 yds / 212m per 100g skein]; color: Melon; 1 skein
- 1 set US #6 / 4mm needles, or size needed to obtain gauge
- Tapestry needle
- Scissors
- Row counter or stitch markers, if desired

Gauge

18 sts / 24 rows = 4" / 10cm in stockinette stitch

Pattern Notes

Included in the pattern directions is a k3 border on each end of the row. These are good places to add stitch markers, if you wish.

Directions

CO 38 sts.
Bottom border: Knit 3 rows.

Row 1 (RS): Knit.
Row 2 (WS): K3, p32, k3.
Row 3: Knit.
Rows 4-10: K3, p32, k3.

Rep this 10-row pattern 6 times, THEN rep Rows 1 & 2 once more.

Top border: Knit 4 rows.

Finishing

BO all sts and weave in all ends.

fresh

This is one of those patterns that remind me of the good ol' days and watching grandma make those fresh, fancy apple pie tops. Fresh conjures up just-cooked bread, crisp vegetables, or an invigorating scent. It's simple, but elegant, and just right for any occasion. You won't even mind scrubbing the pie plate afterwards when you have a lovely dishcloth like this!

Finished Measurements

Approximately 8.5" / 21.5cm square
Note: Dimensions may vary depending on yarn used.

Materials

- Lion Brand Cotton [100% cotton; 236 yds / 216m per 142g skein]; color: Seaspray; 1 skein
- 1 set US #7 / 4.5mm needles, or size needed to obtain gauge
- Tapestry needle
- Scissors
- Row counter or stitch markers, if desired

Gauge

18 sts / 24 rows = 4" / 10cm in stockinette stitch

Pattern Notes

Caution: This pattern is addictive, and will have you making it for all your friends and family.

Directions

CO 40 sts.
Bottom border: Knit 3 rows.

Row 1 (RS): Knit.
Row 2 (WS): K7, *p5, k9; rep from * to last 5 sts, p5.

Row 3: K5, *p9, k5; rep from * to last 7 sts, p7.
Row 4: Rep Row 2.
Row 5: Rep Row 3.
Row 6: Rep Row 2.
Row 7: Knit.
Row 8: P5, *k9, p5; rep from * to last 7 sts, k7.
Row 9: P7, *k5, p9; rep from * to last 5 sts, k5.
Row 10: Rep Row 8.
Row 11: Rep Row 9.
Row 12: Knit.

Rep this 12-row pattern a total of 5 times.

Top border: Knit 3 rows.

Finishing

BO all sts and weave in all ends.

in style

What's your style? You might start with a basic design inspiration such as Contemporary, Modern, Country, or Traditional. Maybe your look is influenced from cultures around the globe: Tuscan, Indian, Oriental, or French Country. What's in style may not be your style. You may like black and white, but what's hot right now is tangerine. That's OK. There's no reason to follow the crowd—make your own style! This dishcloth can accommodate just about any yarn but I like a strong, bright multicolor like Knit One, Crochet Too's Ty-Dy Cotton.

Finished Measurements

Approximately 9" / 23cm square
Note: Dimensions may vary depending on yarn used.

Materials

- Knit One, Crochet Too Ty-Dy Cotton [100% cotton; 196 yds / 179m per 100g skein]; color: Tropical; 1 skein
- 1 set US #7 / 4.5mm needles, or size needed to obtain gauge
- Tapestry needle
- Scissors
- Row counter or stitch markers, if desired

Gauge

20 sts / 24 rows = 4" / 10cm in stockinette stitch

Pattern Notes

Included in the pattern directions is a k3 border on each end of the row. These are good places to add stitch markers, if you wish.

Directions

CO 43 sts.
Bottom border: Knit 3 rows.

Row 1 (RS) and all RS rows through 9: Knit.
Row 2 (WS): K3, *p2, k3; rep from * to last 5 sts, p2, k3.
Row 4: K3, k1, *p2, k3; rep from * to last 4 sts, p1, k3.
Row 6: K3, k2, *p2, k3; rep from * to last 3 sts, k3.
Row 8: K3, *k3, p2; rep from * to last 5 sts, k2, k3.
Row 10: K3, p1, *k3, p2; rep from * to last 4 sts, k1, k3.

Rep this 10-row pattern 6 times.

Top border: Knit 4 rows.

Finishing

BO all sts and weave in all ends.

textures

mosaic tiles

I've always been drawn to mosaic tiles. Mosaics are an art form assembled with small pieces of glass or stone, but you can also create your own from fabric, or in this case, yarn! Early mosaics in the Roman Empire, Byzantium, and elsewhere were often found on walls and floors. Placing tiny tiles in just the right place to create an amazing mosaic can be complicated... but not in this yarny version!

Finished Measurements

Approximately 6.5" / 16.5cm square
Note: Dimensions may vary depending on yarn used.

Materials

- Tahki Cotton Classic [100% mercerized cotton; 108 yds / 99m per 50g skein]; color: #3449; 1 skein
- 1 set US #7 / 4.5mm needles, or size needed to obtain gauge
- Tapestry needle
- Scissors
- Row counter or stitch markers, if desired

Gauge

16 sts / 24 rows = 4" / 10cm in stockinette stitch

Pattern Notes

This pattern is reversible. There is a k3 border on each end of the row included in pattern directions.

Directions

CO 36 sts.
Bottom border: Knit 4 rows.

Row 1 (RS): K3, *p2, k2; rep from * to last 5 sts, p2, k3.
Row 2 (WS): K3, *k2, p2; rep from * to last 5 sts, k2, k3.
Row 3: K3, [k2, p2] twice, *k4, p2, k2, p2; rep from * to last 5 sts, k2, k3.
Row 4: K3, [p2, k2] twice, *p4, k2, p2, k2; repeat from * to last 5 sts, p2, k3.
Rows 5-8: Rep Rows 1-4.
Row 9: Rep Row 1.
Row 10: Rep Row 2.
Row 11: Rep Row 2.
Row 12: Rep Row 1.
Row 13: Rep Row 3.
Row 14: Rep Row 4.
Row 15: Rep Row 2.
Row 16: Rep Row 1.
Row 17: Rep Row 3.
Row 18: Rep Row 4.
Row 19: Rep Row 2.
Row 20: Rep Row 1.

Rep this 20-row pattern once more.

Top border: Knit 3 rows.

Finishing

BO all sts and weave in all ends.

natural

This pattern resembles strands of bamboo, a plant that grows well in many settings, and it is also reminiscent of wicker furniture and of baskets. Adding plants and man-made items inspired by nature lends energy and warmth to modern interior styles. In keeping with current green-living and conservation trends, this long-lasting, natural looking dishcloth can replace disposable sponges and plastic scrubbies, and remind us of the importance of permanent forces in our lives—family and friends.

Finished Measurements

Approximately 6.25" / 16cm
Note: Dimensions may vary depending on yarn used.

Materials

- Universal Yarn Cotton Supreme [100% cotton; 180 yds / 165m per 100g skein]; color: Dutch Blue; 1 skein
- 1 set US #7 / 4.5mm needles, or size needed to obtain gauge
- Tapestry needle
- Scissors
- Row counter or stitch markers, if desired
- Cable needle

Gauge

18 sts / 24 rows = 4" / 10cm in stockinette stitch

Pattern Notes

There is a k3 border on each end of the row included in the pattern directions.

A row counter is helpful with this pattern.

Keeping your cables a bit looser will work well in the overall look of the pattern.

C6B: Slip next 3 sts onto cn and hold yarn in back, k3 from LH needle, then knit the 3 sts from cn.

C6F: Slip next 3 sts onto cn and hold yarn in front, k3 from LH needle, then knit the 3 sts from cn.

Directions

CO 42 sts.
Bottom border: Knit 3 rows.

Row 1 (RS): Knit.
Rows 2, 4, 6, & 8 (WS): K3, p36, k3.
Row 3: K3, k3, *C6B; rep from * to last 6 sts, k3, k3.
Row 5: Knit.
Row 7: K3, *C6F; rep from * to last 3 sts, k3.

Work this 8-row pattern a total of 5 times.

Top border: Knit 4 rows.

Finishing

BO all sts and weave in all ends.

glamour

What comes to mind when you think of glamour in modern design? I know, me too! Satin fabrics, precious metals, brilliant chandeliers, and daring color palettes. Whether it's sparkly mosaic centerpieces that twinkle when the light hits them or a brilliant chandelier hovering over a glass dining room table, glamour is what you make of it. I challenge you to go find a bit of glamour in your decorating style! This shiny, Art Deco-inspired dishcloth will have you dancing like Ginger Rogers...even when Fred sticks you with the dishes.

Finished Measurements

Approximately 8.25" / 21cm square
Note: Dimensions may vary depending on yarn used.

Materials

- Rowan Handknit Cotton [100% cotton; 93 yds / 85m per 50g skein]; color: #330; 1 skein
- 1 set US #7 / 4.5mm needles, or size needed to obtain gauge
- Tapestry needle
- Scissors
- Row counter or stitch markers, if desired

Gauge

18 sts / 24 rows = 4" / 10cm in stockinette stitch

Pattern Notes

There is a k2 border before and after each row included in the pattern directions.

Read through all instructions before beginning pattern. Pay close attention to the rows 3, 5 and 7, where you will p2tog at the end instead of a p3tog. Only the bottom edge of the pattern is scalloped.

Directions

CO 41 sts.
Bottom border: Knit 3 rows.

Row 1 (RS): K2, p1, *p3, k5, p4; rep from * to last 2 sts, k2.
Row 2 and all WS rows: K2, p37, k2.
Row 3: K2, p2tog, *p2, k2, yo, k1, yo, k2, p2, p3tog; rep from * to last 4 sts, p2tog, k2.
Row 5: K2, p2tog, *p1, k2, yo, k3, yo, k2, p1, p3tog; rep from * to last 4 sts, p2tog, k2.
Row 7: K2, p2tog, *k2, yo, k5, yo, k2, p3tog; rep from * to last 4 sts, p2tog, k2.
Row 8: K2, p37, k2.

Rep this 8-row pattern 6 times THEN rows 1-3 once more.

Top border: Knit 3 rows.

Finishing

BO all sts and weave in all ends.

organic

Organic designs are serene and balanced, with clean textures and patterns. And there's nothing like organic cotton: no chemicals, low impact on the environment—the perfect addition to any knitter's yarn stash. This pattern has a modern, natural texture that brings a simple, understated beauty into your kitchen.

Finished Measurements

Approximately 7.5" / 19cm square
Note: Dimensions may vary depending on yarn used.

Materials

- Malabrigo 100% Organic Cotton [100% organic cotton; 232 yds / 212m per 100 g skein]; color: Mandarina; 1 skein
- 1 set US #7 / 4.5mm needles, or size needed to obtain gauge
- Tapestry needle
- Scissors
- Row counter or stitch markers, if desired

Gauge

20 sts / 24 rows = 4" / 10cm in stockinette stitch

Pattern Notes

This pattern is reversible. One must be able to identify a knit and purl stitch on the WS rows. Hint: when working on WS rows, follow the pattern backward (knit the knits, purl the purls).

There is a k3 border on each end of row included in pattern directions.

Directions

CO 38 sts.
Bottom border: Knit 3 rows.

Row 1 (RS): K3, *k1, p1, k1, p5; rep from * to last 3 sts, k3.
Row 2 and all WS rows: K3, knit the K sts and purl the P sts, k3.
Row 3: K3, k1, p1, *k5, p1, k1, p1; rep from * to last 9 sts, k5, p1, k3.
Row 5: K3, k1, *p5, k1, p1, k1; rep from * to last 10 sts, p5, k1, p1, k3.
Row 7: K3, *k5, p1, k1, p1; rep from * to last 3 sts, k3.
Row 9: K3, p4, *k1, p1, k1, p5; rep from * to last 7 sts, [k1, p1] twice, k3.
Row 11: K3, k3, *p1, k1, p1, k5; rep from * to last 8 sts, p1, k1, p1, k2, k3.
Row 13: K3, p2, *k1, p1, k1, p5; rep from * to last 9 sts, k1, p1, k1, p3, k3.
Row 15: K3, k1, *p1, k1, p1, k5; rep from * to last 10 sts, p1, k1, p1, k4, k3.

Rep this 16-row pattern 3 times.

Top border: Knit 3 rows.

Finishing

BO all sts and weave in all ends.

cutting edge

I learned long ago to allow your senses to tell the story when writing—why not do the same with decorating? Use all five senses to create a more powerful style; sight, smell, taste, sound, and touch are textures we can create with our decorating choices. When you place bold textures into your design, you breathe new life into your décor. You heighten the flavor, so to speak. Texture adds sensory interest to a room. This is another pattern that would make a great scarf, if knit longer.

Finished Measurements

Approximately 7.5" / 19cm square
Note: Dimensions may vary depending on yarn used.

Materials

- KnitPicks Dishie [100% cotton; 190 yds / 174m per 100g skein]; color: Honeydew; 1 skein
- 1 set US #7 / 4.5mm needles, or size needed to obtain gauge
- Tapestry needle
- Scissors
- Row counter or stitch markers, if desired

Gauge

18 sts / 24 rows = 4" / 10cm in stockinette stitch

Pattern Notes

There is a k3 border on each end of the row included in the pattern directions.

A row counter is helpful with this pattern.

Directions

CO 35 sts.
Bottom border: Knit 3 rows.

Row 1 (RS): K3, [k1, p2] twice, k3, p11, k3, [p2, k1] twice, k3.
Rows 2 & 16 (WS): K3, k1, [p1, k2] twice, p3, k9, p3, [k2, p1] twice, k1, k3.
Rows 3 & 15: K3, [p2, k1] twice, p2, k3, p7, k3, [p2, k1] twice, p2, k3.
Rows 4 & 14: K3, [p1, k2] three times, p3, k5, p3, [k2, p1] three times, k3.
Rows 5 & 13: K3, k2, [p2, k1] twice, p2, k3, p3, k3, [p2, k1] twice, p2, k2, k3.
Rows 6 & 12: K3, p3, [k2, p1] twice, k2, p3, k1, p3, [k2, p1] twice, k2, p3, k3.
Rows 7 & 11: K3, k4, [p2, k1] twice, p2, k5, [p2, k1] twice, p2, k4, k3.
Rows 8 & 10: K3, p5, [k2, p1] twice, k2, p3, [k2, p1] twice, k2, p5, k3.
Row 9: K3, k6, [p2, k1] five times, p2, k6, k3.

Rep this 16-row pattern 3 times.

Top border: Knit 4 rows.

Finishing

BO all sts and weave in all ends.

Abbreviations

BO	bind off
cn	cable needle
CO	cast on
k	knit
kfb	knit into the front and back of the next stitch
k2tog	knit two stitches together
LH	left-hand
p	purl
p2tog	purl two stitches together
p3tog	purl three stitches together
rep	repeat
RS	right side
skp	slip stitch knitwise, k1, pass slipped stitch over
sl	slip
st(s)	stitch(es)
tbl	through the back loop
w&t	wrap and turn
WS	wrong side
wyib	with yarn in back
yb	bring yarn to back of work
yf	bring yarn to front of work
yo	yarn over

About the Author

After a long day as a certified nurse's aide, Deb Buckingham found that she enjoyed nothing more than to sit down to knit a simple, satisfying dishcloth. Sound familiar?

She is now a full-time knitting pattern designer, and has been published in the *2013 Knitting Calendar* released by Simon and Schuster. Deb is an established designer on Knit Picks as well as on Ravelry. She loves to amuse readers by engaging them in top-ten lists and designer interviews on her blog, theartfulyarn.blogspot.com.

Thanks to...

Dale, my husband, my forever friend, and partner in life, for giving me the push when I didn't want it; for allowing me the luxury to pursue my dream of being an author; for aiding me in prop selection and giving his advice when I didn't think I needed it; for driving me miles away to a yarn shop that "I just had to go to." His unselfish ways in helping me with anything I ask and giving me the go ahead to do what I need to do, are why I love him so unconditionally. I couldn't ask for a kinder, more loving person as my life-long partner.

My precious girls, Jennifer and Christine, for putting up with me while I knit during family conversations, and for being my extra support system; they give me what I need on a daily basis through their kind words and hugs.

Dave and Carol, my loving, amazing parents, who so graciously told me, "you can do it." Their words of "we are so proud of you" ring in my ears every day. I'm over the moon with the support I receive from the two of them.

My sisters Kellie and Michele, for allowing me to bounce ideas off, and share in my excitement. Their loving approach is always a piece of sunshine in my day.

Pam, for her persistent nudge that gave me the courage to figure out how to be a designer—for that, I will always be grateful.

My knitsters—my fabulous test knitters, my Bitch 'n Knit girls, whom I will forever be thankful for… Jackie, who taught me to back out of an "oops" by going back through the same hole you came through. Tish, who is forever coming up with ideas for anything I throw out there. Julia for being her sweet self in offering to help in any way she can. Rainae is the one person who always has a story and willing to help. Marty, who would give me the shirt off her back (if it wasn't pink) and be honest with her answers. Anna is the one who says, "Done. Got another?" Cathy, Lori, Pam, Pat, and Michele who graciously offered their time to help with the project. Rachel, whose wisdom brought my descriptions from drab to fab. You all rock!

Ann, for allowing me the use of her kitchen.

Nemo's Coffee, for allowing me to sit for hours while I edit photos, write pages, or just knit while sipping coffee. JD and Tracy are the most amazing people when it comes to their sincerity, generosity, and are oh-so-totally cool.

Yarn Contributors

Tahki Stacy Charles

www.tahkistacycharles.com

Universal Yarn

www.universalyarns.com

Knit One, Crochet Too

www.knitonecrochettoo.com

KnitPicks

www.knitpicks.com

Malabrigo

www.malabrigoyarn.com

Classic Elite Yarns

www.classiceliteyarns.com

About Cooperative Press

Cooperative Press (formerly anezka media) was founded in 2007 by Shannon Okey, a voracious reader as well as writer and editor, who had been doing freelance acquisitions work, introducing authors with projects she believed in to editors at various publishers.

Although working with traditional publishers can be very rewarding, there are some books that fly under their radar. They're too avant-garde, or the marketing department doesn't know how to sell them, or they don't think they'll sell 50,000 copies in a year.

5,000 or 50,000. Does the book matter to that 5,000? Then it should be published.

In 2009, Cooperative Press changed its named to reflect the relationships we have developed with authors working on books. We work together to put out the best quality books we can and share in the proceeds accordingly.

Thank you for supporting independent publishers and authors.

Join our mailing list for information on upcoming books!

www.cooperativepress.com

CPSIA information can be obtained at www.ICGtesting.com
Printed in the USA
BVOW10s2141130514

353432BV00003B/24/P